Meet the Octopus

by Sylvia M. James
illustrated by Cynthia A. Belcher

Sylvia M. James is the Director of Education Programs at the
National Aquarium in Baltimore, located in Baltimore, Maryland.

Photograph Credits Kevin and Cat Sweeney/Tony Stone Images: p. 4; © Mike
Severns: p. 9 right; © Fred McConnaughey, The National Audobon Society
Collection/Photo Researchers: p. 9 left; © Geo. Lower, The National Audobon
Society Collection/Photo Researchers: p. 17; © Corp. R. Stuart Westmorland,
The National Audobon Society Collection/Photo Researchers; p. 19.

Designed by PCI Design Group, San Antonio, Texas

Printed in China
02 03 04   9 8 7

ISBN 1-57255-120-8

Contents

What Is an Octopus?

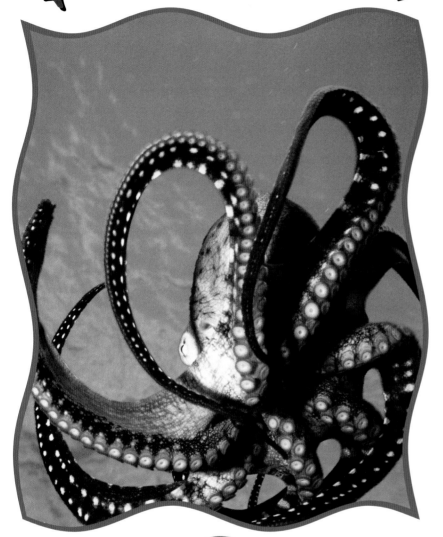

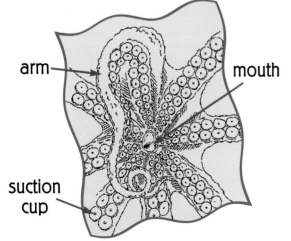

arm

mouth

suction cup

An octopus is an animal that lives in the sea. Its body is like a soft, wrinkled sac with eight long arms. Its mouth is in the middle of the arms, and there are two rows of sticky suction cups on each arm.

There are 150 kinds of octopuses. Some are very small. Others are huge.

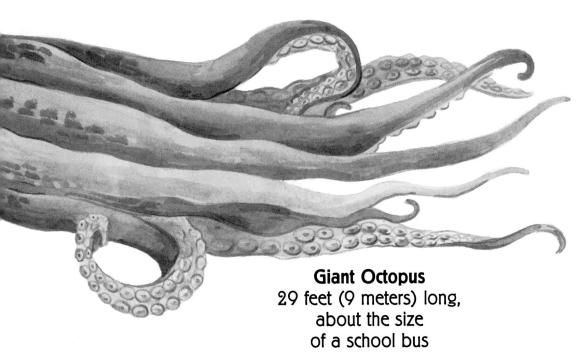

Giant Octopus
29 feet (9 meters) long,
about the size
of a school bus

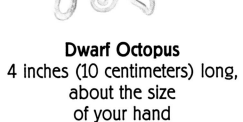

Dwarf Octopus
4 inches (10 centimeters) long,
about the size
of your hand

Common Octopus
10 feet (3 meters) long,
about the size
of a station wagon

Hiding and Escaping

An octopus' body is soft and
has no bones. It can become flat
and squeeze through tight spaces.

An octopus has many ways of hiding. It can hide among rocks.

Can you find an octopus hiding in this picture?

An octopus can also change color
to match the things around it. It may
turn brown, red, yellow, or blue to
look like seaweed or coral. This makes
the octopus hard to see.

An octopus can even look like
a bumpy rock.

Can you find the octopuses on these pages?

Sometimes other animals try to
eat the octopus. But the octopus
has a special trick for escaping. It
shoots a cloud of black ink out of
its body so the enemy cannot see
and smell.

The ink cloud may even look like an octopus. The enemy is fooled and attacks the ink cloud. This gives the octopus a chance to get away.

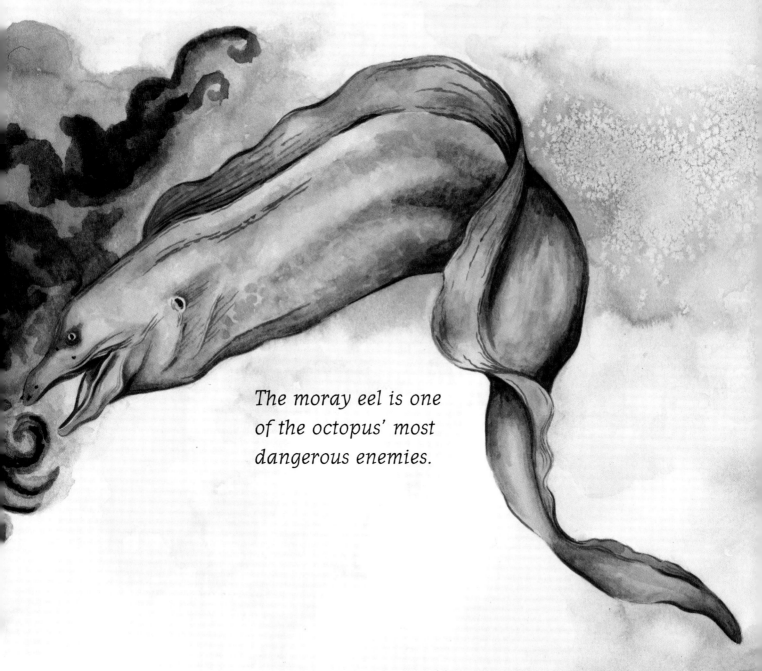

The moray eel is one of the octopus' most dangerous enemies.

The octopus can get away fast! It shoots jets of water out of its body, which make the octopus move quickly in the sea. *Whoosh!*

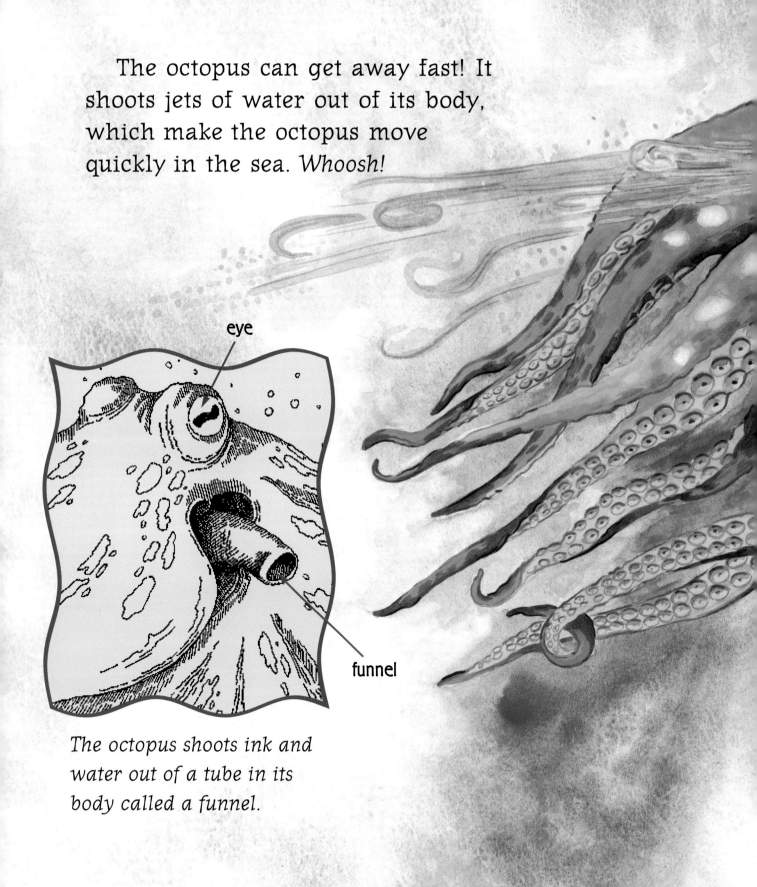

eye

funnel

The octopus shoots ink and water out of a tube in its body called a funnel.

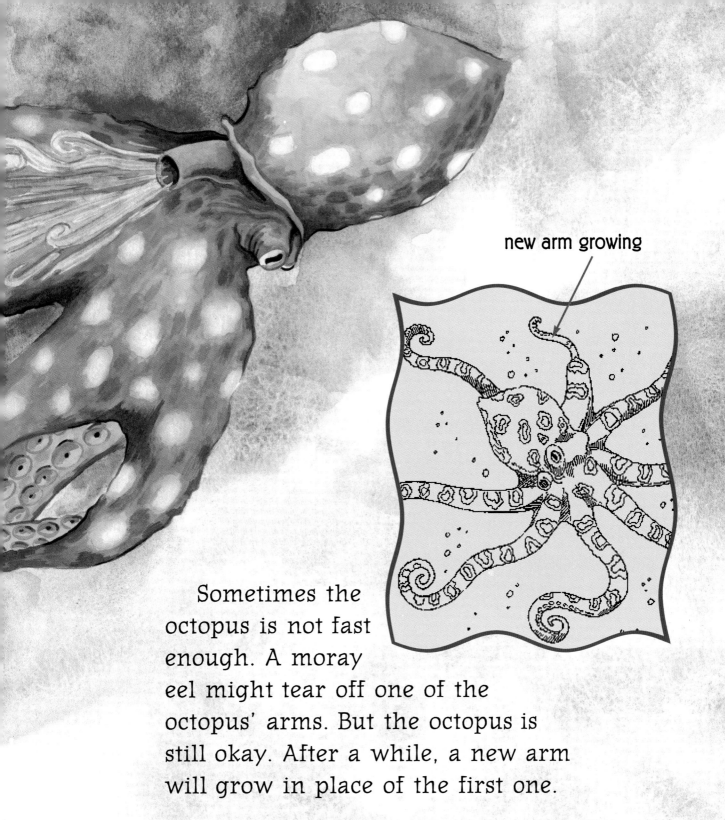

new arm growing

Sometimes the octopus is not fast enough. A moray eel might tear off one of the octopus' arms. But the octopus is still okay. After a while, a new arm will grow in place of the first one.

Where the Octopus Lives

This octopus has made its den in some rocks.

An octopus finds a special home in the sea where it hides, rests, and eats. The octopus' home is called a den.

Getting Food

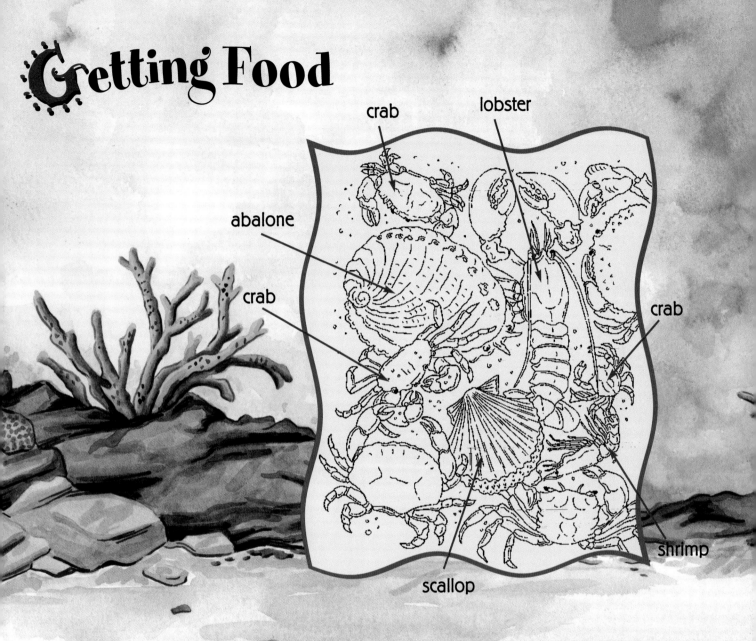

crab

lobster

abalone

crab

crab

scallop

shrimp

The octopus stays in its den during the day. At night, the octopus hunts for food. Its favorite foods are crabs, lobsters, shrimp, and scallops.

Most of the time, the octopus crawls along the ocean floor using its arms to feel and grab things. The octopus also stretches out its arms to reach for food.

suction cup

The common octopus has 240 suction cups on each arm. The suction cups help the octopus move and feed.

When the octopus finds a crab, it pounces on it and covers the crab with its arms. Then the octopus squirts poison into the crab. The poison makes the crab stop moving.

Now the octopus uses its strong beak to crack the crab shell. Then the octopus eats the meat inside.

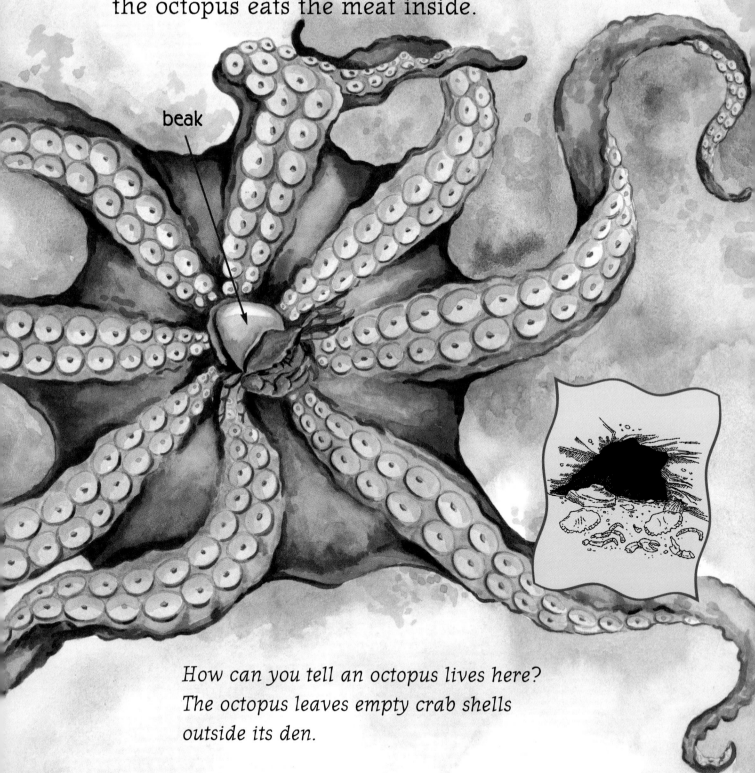

beak

How can you tell an octopus lives here? The octopus leaves empty crab shells outside its den.

Octopus Babies

Some octopuses lay as many as 200,000 eggs.

The female giant Pacific octopus lays thousands of eggs which look like grains of rice. The octopus strings these eggs together and hangs them in her den.

The octopus never leaves her eggs. She does not even eat or hunt for food.

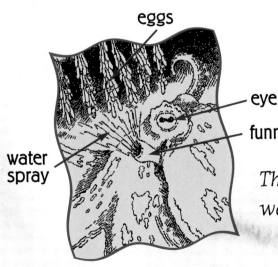

eggs

eye

funnel

water spray

The octopus sprays her eggs with water to keep them clean.

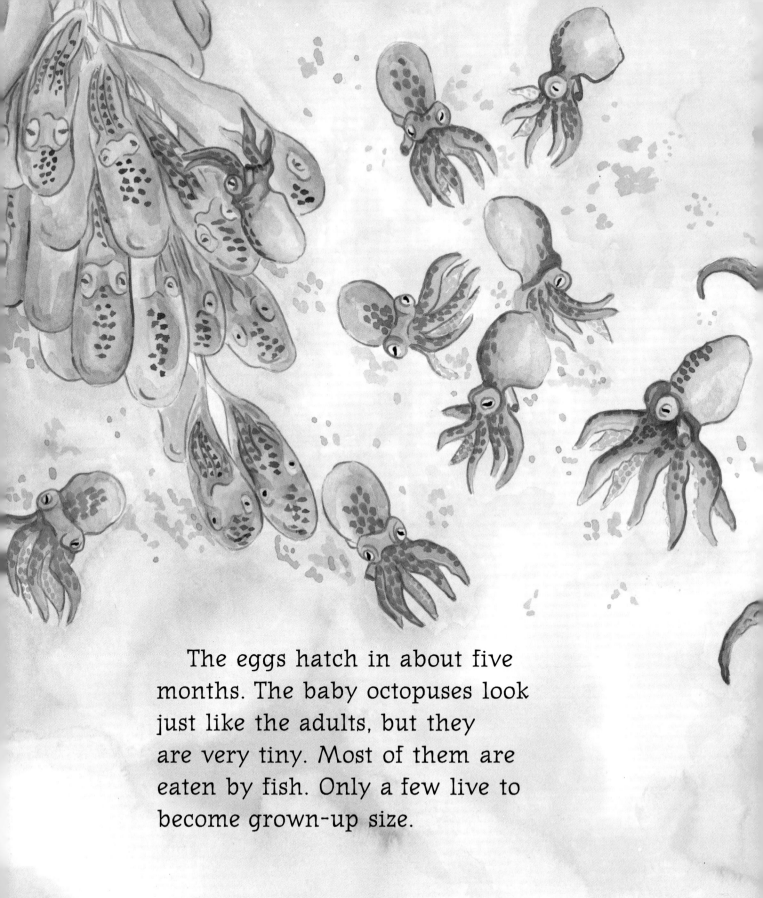

The eggs hatch in about five
months. The baby octopuses look
just like the adults, but they
are very tiny. Most of them are
eaten by fish. Only a few live to
become grown-up size.

The babies grow slowly for the first two years. Then they grow very quickly. Most octopuses live for only three or four years.

What Scientists Have Learned

Scientists have studied the octopus for many years. These are some of the things they have learned.

- The octopus eye is almost the same as the human eye.

- The octopus sees very well, but it cannot see in color.

- The octopus cannot hear.

- The octopus can learn to recognize shapes.

- The octopus can solve problems such as opening a jar.

Index